The
Hard Hat

21 Ways to Be a Great Teammate

A True Story

The Heart of a Leader and the
Spirit of a Team

JON GORDON

WILEY

Published by John Wiley & Sons, Inc., Hoboken, New Jersey.
Published simultaneously in Canada.

For general information about our other products and services, please contact our Customer Care Department within the United States at (800) 762-2974, outside the United States at (317) 572-3993 or fax (317) 572-4002.

Wiley publishes in a variety of print and electronic formats and by print-on-demand. Some material included with standard print versions of this book may not be included in e-books or in print-on-demand. If this book refers to media such as a CD or DVD that is not included in the version you purchased, you may download this material at http://booksupport.wiley.com. For more information about Wiley products, visit www.wiley.com.

Library of Congress Cataloging-in-Publication Data:
Gordon, Jon, 1971-
    The hard hat : 21 ways to be a great teammate / Jon Gordon.
        pages cm
    ISBN 978-1-119-12011-7 (hardback); ISBN 978-1-119-12012-4 (ebk);
ISBN 978-1-119-12013-1 (ebk)
    1. Teams in the workplace. 2. Motivation (Psychology) I. Title.
    HD66.G672 2015
    650.1'3–dc23   2015008091

Printed in the United States of America.

SKY10057534_101223

This book is dedicated to the 2004 Cornell Lacrosse Team. Your character, resilience, heart, determination, and love for George and each other made this book possible. Without you there wouldn't be a story to tell and I'm thankful you shared your experiences and memories with me.

Contents

Contents

Part Four Legacy   **77**

Contents

Foreword

I remember hearing the news. The captain of Cornell's lacrosse team had died, on the field of play, after getting hit in the chest with a ball. How terrible, how cruel, how utterly tragic. What else could you think? As a Cornell graduate, with a connection to the lacrosse program, perhaps I felt all those things more acutely than most people who came across the news in their newspaper or on the Internet. In a way, the death was more real to me because I had grown up around Cornell lacrosse, I knew Cornell lacrosse players, and I understood how tight knit that community had always been.

Just two years earlier, in my role as a reporter at ESPN, I had written a tribute to the life of another Cornell lacrosse captain who had died too young, but not nearly as young as George Boiardi. Eamon McEneaney, one of the sport's great figures, had died on September 11, 2001, at the World Trade Center, where he worked in finance. When attending his funeral in New Canaan, Connecticut, I witnessed an outpouring of emotion that stays with me even now. Richie Moran, Cornell's longtime head coach, a man I had known all my life, eulogized McEneaney. Totally overcome, he barely made it through his tribute. I have never seen a grown man or woman so unhinged by grief. He was sobbing, and his pain was so pure that everyone in the church could feel it. It was beautiful and awful—an unforgettable coda to a week unlike any other in New York. It was also indicative of the way in which Cornell lacrosse is a family. The current team was there, McEneaney's old teammates were there, and the network of friends and acquaintances he had made through lacrosse were all there.

Then George died on St. Patrick's Day, 2004. That was cruel, too—not because George was of Irish extraction, but because Moran and McEneaney and so many others in the Cornell lacrosse community were. I had never met George. I don't think I had ever heard his name until the day he died, although I assumed we had been together at McEneaney's funeral. But over the next several years, I would come to know George—through his family and friends, at the events they held to honor his memory and to raise money to benefit causes that were meaningful to him.

Every winter since then, a dinner is held in New York—the 21 Dinner, in recognition of his uniform number—and hundreds of George's friends, from home and from Cornell, would attend. There was nothing extraordinary about the gesture. Naturally, people close to George would want to celebrate his life and find a way to remember him. But the dinners—organized primarily by George's Cornell classmate and friend, Jesse Rothstein—would turn out to be anything but ordinary. Even as they embarked on their careers and started their busy post-college lives, George's friends would come together every winter—it seemed always to fall on the coldest night of the year—to remember George. I have been a part of other efforts to memorialize fallen friends; often, attendance and interest are strong in the first few years after the friend has died, then they decline, memories fade, and people move on. That wasn't the case with George. With each passing year, it seemed the determination to keep his spirit alive only strengthened among those he had left behind.

I came to look forward to the event—to seeing George's parents and sisters, his friends and teammates, the honorees from the world of education, to which George had pledged himself as a Teach for America volunteer. At one of the dinners, representatives of the Native American reservation on which George was going to teach were in attendance. They came to pay their respects to the young man who had grown up in a world of privilege but had decided to live among them in very different circumstances for at least a couple of years.

It seems too easy to say, but my faith in humanity was always restored by the 21 Dinner. It was also made meaningful to me by the organizers, who honored my father at the event. Like George, he had worn number 21 playing lacrosse for Cornell. He had died on December 21, 2001, in New York, after hip surgery at the age of 67—too young, but old enough to have lived a full, rewarding life, which George had been denied.

Seeing George so fondly and well remembered at the dinners—I was a mostly superfluous master of ceremonies each year—I felt as if I came to understand why he meant so much to so many. The way people talked about him, I think I could draw a fairly accurate portrait of a young man with so much to offer. There was the selflessness, the work ethic, the kindness, the gentlemanliness, and a total lack of arrogance or sense of entitlement. He seemed to be exactly the kind of person we could all respect—someone Eamon McEneaney, my father and I, and anyone else would have considered themselves privileged to have known. Of course, not having met George, there is still much I didn't know about him. This book remedies that. Clearly, he was someone worth knowing.

—Jeremy Schaap

Author's Note

From the moment I first heard about George Boiardi and the Hard Hat I was intrigued and captivated. I wanted to know more about him and his life. I visited his coaches, attended several "21 Dinners" held in his honor, met his family, talked to his teammates, and personally observed how he inspired all who knew him. I never intended to write a book about him but the more I learned, the more I felt compelled to share the kind of teammate he was and the impact he had on others.

Yet, as I began to write this book several times over the years, I stopped. As someone who writes fables, not true stories, I knew it would be uncomfortable and challenging to interview his family, friends, coaches, and teammates and write a story filled with actual events, laughable moments, painful emotions, and an unforgettable tragedy. But I couldn't walk away from it. I knew that everything in my life had brought me to this moment where I was meant to write about and share George's lessons and legacy with others. So I stepped out of my comfort zone and did my best to tell a true story about how to be a great teammate.

Please know that this is just a small part of the whole story of George's life. He was so much more than just a teammate. He was a son, friend, brother, nephew, and student, and only his family and friends could tell the whole story.

My goal in writing this book was to share the characteristics that made George a great teammate and inspire others to be better people and teammates as well. As I interviewed many of George's friends and teammates, I also realized that this was more than just a book about him; it was also about them. In the face of the worst tragedy of their lives, they found a way to come together, heal, and play selflessly and purposefully as a team. What the 2004 Cornell Lacrosse team accomplished is truly a testament to their incredible character, resilience, heart, determination, and love for George and each other. Without these young men there wouldn't be a story to tell, and I'm thankful they shared their experiences and memories with me.

All of the details and stories in the book are, to the best of my knowledge, factual and true. In Part 2 of the book it says "Narrated by Coach Jeff Tambroni"; however, I want to be transparent and let the reader know that this section is actually a compilation of numerous recollections, facts, and stories from Jeff, George's family, and teammates. After I conducted all the interviews and began to write the book, I realized that having one narrator would make George's story flow better and create a better experience for the reader. Jeff really did tell me about George in a meeting as I described in the book; however, I had to rely on his teammates and family to learn more details and tell a complete story. In addition to learning about George and his teammates at the 21 Dinners and Hall of Fame Dinner, I conducted a number of interviews via phone and email as well.

During the writing process I shared the manuscript with Jeff Tambroni and George's family and teammates several times to make sure all the facts were accurate. The book really was a team effort and I hope it inspires and impacts you and your team.

Part One

The Hard Hat

Chapter 1

Unforgettable

When you see something for the first time, you never forget it. As I write this, I can still picture the 2007 semi-final game of the NCAA Men's Lacrosse Championships between Cornell and Duke. Duke was leading 10–3 in the third quarter and all seemed lost for Cornell. But with unparalleled determination, Cornell staged a furious comeback and tied Duke with 17 seconds left in the game. Duke would eventually win by scoring a goal with three seconds left, showing their own fortitude, but it was the comeback and effort by Cornell that left me in awe.

I played lacrosse at Cornell in the early nineties and had also watched thousands of games in numerous sports, but I had never seen a team play with such spirit, passion, grit, resilience, and relentless determination as Cornell did in the second half of that game. Since I work with many professional and college sports teams as well as teams in the corporate, educational, and non-profit world, I had to find out what inspired this team to play the way they did. As a student and teacher of human motivation, I knew it had to be more than a desire to win. They were driven by something much bigger and I was very curious to discover what it was.

So, I went on a quest back to the place where I spent my college years, a place that shaped and molded me in so many ways. On the plane to upstate New York, I realized that I could connect the work I did now with many of the growth opportunities I experienced as a student-athlete. Playing a sport in college changed my life forever and taught me to work hard; overcome adversity, rejection, self-doubts, and fears; and keep striving toward my dreams. I left as a student, became a teacher, and landed at the Ithaca airport ready to be a student again. As I arrived on the campus I hadn't seen in over 10 years, I felt a familiar chill in the October air and I was prepared to learn new lessons on leadership and teamwork.

Chapter 2

We Know Who Our People Are

I found Jeff Tambroni, the Cornell men's lacrosse coach, standing on the sidewalk by the lacrosse office as I walked up the hill from the Statler Hotel. I had played against Jeff in college when he was an All-American attackman at Hobart College and I was a face-off man and defensive midfielder for Cornell. I could still picture the way he looked back then and remembered his incredible quickness and uncanny ability to create scoring opportunities for his team. Unfortunately, it had happened against Cornell and me far too many times.

My time at Cornell is regrettably called the beginning of the dark years. Before I had joined the team, Cornell had made it to the national championships two years in a row. My sophomore year, we were ranked ninth in the country but, during my senior year, we had the first losing season in the history of legendary Richie Moran's coaching career. The program experienced a number of challenging times and losing seasons in the years following my graduation, but Jeff Tambroni, first as an assistant and then as head coach, had restored Cornell to a lacrosse powerhouse program once again.

When I asked Jeff how he got Cornell back to its winning ways, he said, "We know and embrace who our people are. In years past we would recruit lacrosse players *en masse*, but now we are looking to recruit a specific ten who most appropriately fit our culture. In fact, instead of trying to be everything to everyone, we actually try to weed out the people who wouldn't be a good fit. We highlight the reality of our culture; it's really cold in Ithaca much of the time and if you don't like the cold, this is probably not the right place for you. We let them know it snows a lot during the late fall and winter at Cornell, and if you don't like the snow, this is not the right place for you. We tell them that if they come here, we will provide them with an opportunity to train hard and be one of the hardest-working teams in the country with no illusion of wins and losses. If you don't like to work hard for others, this is not the right place for you. We tell them about the *hard hat*, and if it doesn't resonate with them then we know it won't be a good fit. The hard hat has become a big part of our culture and represents all that we stand for. By weeding out the wrong people, we are able to zero in on the right guys that fit our culture and then partner with them as they develop into great teammates and a great team."

Chapter 3

The Hard Hat

 I was very curious about the hard hat, and asked Jeff what it was all about. He said, "A few years ago we got together as a coaching staff, including our head coach Dave Pietramala, who is currently the head coach at Johns Hopkins, and realized we wanted our culture and program to be defined by our toughness, selflessness, and hard work. Hard hats are usually worn by construction workers, and we decided to use it to symbolize the blue-collar work ethic we wanted our program and teams to possess."

"The idea is that our players will come to practice, punch the clock, and give a blue-collar, workman-like effort every day. We tell them, 'Come to practice, do your job, and work as hard as you can.' To ingrain the hard hat symbol and character traits into our culture, each season we select a freshman to carry the hard hat for the year. The player selected is someone who we feel demonstrates the blue-collar approach to the game of lacrosse. He sets the example for others and is driven and selfless. He may not be the most talented player on the field but is consistently the hardest worker. He puts his team first and embodies how our players are supposed to act on and off the field.

"The player selected to carry the hard hat is expected to bring it to practice and games. We want our guys to look at the bench and see the hard hat. It's in every team picture, as well. We want each young man to see it and remember why he came to *this* university and chose to be a part of *this* program. We want to remind them what we stand for as a team. We want them to live and share our values each day. We want our culture to build them into better men and, in turn, have them continue to build a better culture. Most of all, ever since George, we want the hard hat to remind them to do everything they can to be great teammates. George embodied everything the hard hat stood for, and now the hard hat embodies the teammate and person George was. You can't talk about the hard hat without talking about George, and you can't talk about George without talking about the hard hat. They have become inseparable."

I saw tears well up in Jeff's eyes as he spoke about George and wanted to hear more, but didn't want to pry. I could tell there was a lot more to the story, so I was thankful when he walked me into his office, showed me a picture of George, and said, "You want to know why we have become the program we have, let me tell you about the heart of a leader and the spirit of a team. Let me tell you about the greatest teammate I have ever played with or had the honor to coach. Let me tell you about George."

Part Two

George

Narrated by Coach Jeff Tambroni

Chapter 4

Mario St. George Boiardi

 His name was Mario St. George Boiardi but everyone called him George. I can still remember the first time our coaching staff saw him. I was an assistant coach standing on the sidelines with Coach Pietramala at a high school recruiting tournament. George was on the wing getting ready for a face-off and we couldn't take our eyes off of him. He had cut-off sleeves, sculpted arms, and looked like a fierce warrior getting ready to do battle. He wasn't a bulky guy but he was tall, athletic, and fit. He had a warrior spirit that drew you to him. We never saw a guy run faster and harder to the ball. He moved swiftly like a deer, but if you got in his way he would hit you like a truck. He was one of the top long-stick midfielders in the country, and we wanted him on our team.

When our staff met George for the first time, we were surprised because he was nothing like we expected. Off the field, this warrior was soft-spoken, quiet, and humble. When Coach Pietramala and I visited his house, we asked his parents about George's quiet demeanor. His mom, Deborah, went upstairs and brought down a paperweight that sat on George's nightstand. It was a gift from his father, Mario, and it had a quote from Benjamin Franklin on it: "Well done is better than well said." She told us this is who George is. He is a quiet leader. He doesn't talk a lot; he speaks through his actions. Little did we know at the time how much his actions would tell us.

The fact that George chose to attend Cornell was a complete surprise to everyone. His father was a graduate of Princeton, and their coach really wanted George to play for their team. They were one of the top teams in the country at the time, so everyone assumed George had locked in Princeton as his first choice. Even so, George came on a recruiting visit to Cornell and stayed with Billy Fort, one of his old high school classmates from the Landon School in Maryland. We had a rule on our team that if you were a player hosting a recruit, you had to give the recruit your bed while you slept on the couch or the floor. During George's visit, Billy gave George his bed and didn't think much of it. In fact, he didn't think it mattered at all. The players knew that a bed wouldn't be a deciding factor for any recruit. Guys at that age are thinking about other things while visiting a college. But for George it mattered. He told his parents that it was a sign to him that Cornell really wanted him there. He was impressed by the gesture and thought it said a lot about the culture and team we were building. Most young men at that age don't think like that, but that's the kind of person George was. He was different, and, to him, actions mattered.

Chapter 5

Well Done Is Better than Well Said

No one, as a freshman, worked harder in the weight room than George. No one ran harder during conditioning drills. Everything he did was to the best of his ability. He was one of the most competitive players we had ever seen, but he wasn't driven by the need to be better than anyone else. He just wanted to be the best *he* could be and always drove himself to improve. He was one of the best young players we had, but he worked and trained like a walk-on trying to make the team. He set the example and led the way in everything he did—even with our team traditions.

Our team had a tradition that after the first captain's practice of the fall semester (NCAA rules don't allow coaches to be there), the team would take a run around campus. Freshmen love this because it's one of their first times wearing the Cornell practice gear and they have a chance to run through campus and be seen by the student body. The team ran in two lines, seniors in the front, followed by juniors and sophomores, with freshmen at the end of the line. At the end of the run, the players cross over a footbridge off of Forest Home Drive, about 30 or 40 feet above Beebe Lake. As the last sophomore crosses the bridge, the upperclassmen stop and surprise the freshmen, letting them know that it's a tradition for freshmen to jump into the lake.

Some freshmen immediately jump, others take a little encouragement, and some need convincing. After more and more of the guys jumped into the lake, there were two left who were visibly nervous. As the story goes, George quietly spoke to them, letting them know it wasn't a big deal as they nodded their heads in unison. Next thing you know George climbs up on the rock ledge and jumps head first into the water. In mid-air George, with his head leading the fall, takes his two arms and grabs his feet, and at the last second, he tucks into a perfect dive and leaves no splash, like something you see in the Olympics. It turns out George wasn't just a great lacrosse player; as a boy he was also a great swimmer and diver.

The final two players immediately climbed up to the ledge and, with the team cheering, jumped in, hand-and-hand. The three of them climbed out of the lake together. George knew the two guys were scared and uncomfortable, so he did what great leaders do. He went first and led the way.

Chapter 6

Chosen

 George was chosen to carry the hard hat at the end of the fall practice season. It wasn't an honor he had sought; it was one he had earned. George never wanted credit for anything. He didn't care about personal statistics. He was the guy who would pick up a ground ball and pass it to a teammate who would pass it again to someone else who would take the shot and score. He worked so hard and was so selfless that people gravitated to him as a leader. He had moral authority because he did everything the right way. He never slacked and never took a play off in practice or games. Yes, the guys were in awe of his athletic ability, but it was his work ethic and selflessness that earned their respect and admiration.

The coaching staff asked George to switch from being a long-stick defensive midfielder to a short-stick defensive mid-fielder because we already had one of the best long-stick midfielders in the country, a junior named Josh Heller. We figured if we could get George and Josh on the field at the same time, we would be that much better. But we also knew it wasn't an easy transition for George to make. Playing with a short stick versus a long stick requires a completely different set of stick skills and would present a huge challenge. When we asked

George to switch, he didn't complain at all. In fact, it still amazes me that here he was, one of the top recruits in the country as a long-stick midfielder, and he was willing to switch in order to make the team better.

Instead of complaining to his coaches and teammates, George focused on improving. Every day for the rest of the year George would be out there before and after practice throwing the ball against the wall, working to improve his stick skills. The guys on the team would tease George that he was the greatest athlete with the worst stick skills of all time, but George didn't listen to any of it. All he was focused on was getting better. I can remember many freezing nights, long after practice was over—his teammates were taking warm showers—and I'd see George out there throwing the ball against the wall. And I wasn't the only one who noticed. Everyone saw George putting in extra time and it spoke volumes about who he was and what he was all about.

Guys worked hard because they knew George was working hard. He pushed everyone to work harder and get better without saying a word. He didn't have to. They saw how he went about his business. Even the older players on the team looked up to him.

The Hard Hat

Chapter 7

Selfless Leadership

 When young adults come to college, they often change. They reinvent themselves, evolve, or mature into different people than they were in high school. But the interesting thing about George was that he didn't change at all during his time at Cornell. In fact, he was the same person he had been during his years in high school. Even though he didn't talk a lot, he had powerful eyes that told you what he was feeling and he had a smile that lit up the room. While he was very intense on the field, off the field George had a joyful spirit. He loved life, listening to reggae, and wearing sandals. His parents joked with him that the cold weather at Cornell would make it difficult to wear sandals but George said that even that wouldn't stop him, and it didn't.

As the years went by and our team changed, George and his leadership principles did not. He didn't speak often but when he did everyone listened. They knew if George was speaking he had something significant to say. There was no pretense about him. He was who he was. Humble, sincere, joyful, selfless, and compassionate. He had a very simple, effortless leadership style and approach. He was genuine and always put others before himself.

George always stood up for those who wouldn't stand up for themselves. If someone was teasing a team member or saying something bad about someone, George would say to knock it off. He wouldn't make the person feel bad. He would simply tell them what they were doing was wrong. He joked around but never said a bad word about anyone and wouldn't let others, either. He didn't have a mean bone in his body. He gave everything to his team but never took anything away from anyone. Friends and teammates who knew him when he was younger say he was the same way in high school.

Another practice George started in high school was to be the last person to leave the locker room. He played football, hockey, and lacrosse, and he was always the last to leave. He would clean up after everyone so the janitor didn't have to do it. It was a practice he continued in college as a freshman and throughout his time at Cornell. Whenever you walked into the locker room after practice, you knew George was going to be there. As an upperclassman, he was always the last to leave and, in doing so, he would often drive the freshmen home, knowing they had a long, cold walk ahead of them to North Campus. George always put the team first and looked for ways to serve.

One of my favorite stories is about what happened after a team dinner at a downtown restaurant during George's senior year. A bunch of freshmen needed a ride back to campus. Many of the upperclassmen had already left, so George piled all the remaining freshmen into his old black Jeep Cherokee. On the way back to campus, a cop pulled George's car over. When he approached the car and looked inside, he saw a bunch of people crammed inside and asked them all to get out. One by one the freshmen got out of the car, which took a while because there were so many. The cop laughed and was amazed that they were able to fit 12 guys in the car. But that's how George was; he was there for everyone and wouldn't leave anyone behind.

Chapter 8

A Difference Maker

 George came from a family whose success was based on hard work and helping others, and that was how he lived his life. His team knew that he could always be counted on to help someone else. He would take the shirt off his back and give it to someone in need. George didn't live for himself; he lived for his team and for others. It was no surprise that George was named a captain in his senior year. But George's leadership didn't stop in the locker room or on the field.

When we weren't in season, he volunteered as an assistant to a Little League team on weekends in the Cornell polo barns. He had played baseball and been coached by volunteers when he was a kid, and wanted to give back in the same way.

After the 2004 season started, Ladeen Case, who was the wife of our athletic trainer, Jim Case, and taught at a school in downtown Ithaca, asked me if our players would be interested in reading to elementary school students. George happened to be standing next to me and I asked him if he would set this up. George quickly organized a group of his teammates to read to the students and they planned to make their first visit after our next game.

George wasn't sure what he wanted to do after graduation, but he had started to seriously consider teaching. The desire to teach became stronger after visiting his high school teammate and college friend Brigham Kiplinger, who was a teacher with Teach For America in Washington, DC. George had the opportunity to work with children in Brigham's class during his visit and he was hooked. He officially applied to the Teach For America program with a desire to teach on the Pine Ridge and Rosebud Lakota Sioux reservations in southwestern South Dakota. At Cornell, George was fascinated by the courses he took related to Native American culture and wanted to serve the children there.

George was so excited about this teaching opportunity that he was very nervous he wouldn't be selected for the program. He had to write an essay and go through a formal interview process to be selected. The night before his interview, George went into the room of his friend and teammate Scott Raasch and took a seat in the recliner. Even though he was a man of few words in team settings, he talked more in one-on-one conversations. He shared with Scott how nervous he was about the Teach For America interview the next day. When Scott assured him he had nothing to be nervous about, George explained that he was never comfortable in situations where he had to talk about himself and his accomplishments.

The next day, Scott was walking through campus between classes and bumped into George, who told him he was heading to the interview. When Scott asked him if he was nervous, George responded by raising both arms over his head to reveal two giant, armpit sweat stains showing through his tan suit jacket. Scott and George laughed together before Scott wished him luck and told him he would see him in the locker room before our game that night. A few hours later, another friend and teammate, David Coors, saw George walking down the hill from his interview and asked him how it went. George, in classic fashion, didn't say a word. He just lifted his arms and with a big grin showed David his armpits as well. Neither David nor Scott ever got the chance to talk to George about his interview. When they arrived at the locker room before the game, George was already sitting quietly in front of his locker, intensely focused on one thing: beating our opponent.

The game was supposed to take place the night before, on Tuesday, March 16, but due to snow it had been rescheduled for Wednesday, March 17. As nervous as George had been about his Teach For America interview, he was probably equally nervous about the game that night. It was early in the season, our team hadn't been playing well, and, as a captain, George felt personally responsible. He knew the team was missing something, but he wasn't sure what it was.

Chapter 9

The Heart of a Leader

In the second game of the season our team had suffered an embarrassing loss to Georgetown in Washington, DC, in front of many of George's hometown friends and family. He was really upset about the way our team had played. After that, we won against Stony Brook, but just barely, with the team playing way below our potential. George was relentless in that game, stealing the ball from opposing players, picking up tons of ground balls, running like the wind, doing everything in his power to help lead us to victory.

Before that next game on the 17th, George was pacing around the locker room, and he shared his concerns with his fellow captain, Andrew Collins. He said the team wasn't where we needed to be and he was looking forward to getting us back on track.

It was an intensely cold Wednesday night and our team was once again playing way below its potential. We should have been cruising to victory, but in the fourth quarter we were only leading by a few goals. At this point in the game, George shouldn't have been playing. We should have secured the win so some of the younger guys could have taken the field to gain some experience and playing time. But with the game so close and the outcome uncertain, George was still in the game, playing as relentlessly as ever, trying to deliver a win for our team.

Our opponent had the ball on offense in a man-up situation as they looked for another opportunity to score and move one step closer to tying the game. They took a shot from about 15 yards out, but George jumped in front of the ball and blocked it with his chest. Then, he took a few steps to the sideline, staggered, and fell to the turf. Jim Case, the lacrosse athletic trainer, ran out there immediately, knowing something was seriously wrong. Jim performed CPR for several minutes, until the ambulance came and took George to the hospital where they tried to resuscitate him without success.

It was the worst moment of my life, and one that would define me both as a person and as a coach forever. It was one of the few games George's parents had missed in three and a half years; because it had been rescheduled, they hadn't been able to make it. About 90 minutes after George was taken off the field, we received word from the hospital that he had passed away. After a moment of silent reflection, I called Mr. and Mrs. Boiardi to deliver the news. It was the hardest thing I have ever had to do. Nothing can ever prepare you for that moment. Then I had to tell the team. They were in the locker room waiting and hoping for good news about George. I walked into the locker room with tears in my eyes and had to step back into the coach's office to compose myself before speaking with them. The team just burst into tears, and all you could hear were sobs of sorrow. They were in shock, disbelief, and a lot of pain. They wept together. Their captain, teammate, friend, and the heart of our team was gone.

Chapter 10

A Mother's Touch

George's family raced up to Cornell as fast as they could. They went to see him one last time before coming to talk to the team the next day in the locker room. The guys were all sitting at their lockers just as they did when I shared the news about George. Some were in tears and some were sobbing.

Mrs. Boiardi walked into the locker room with her husband, approached the guys, and, after a long pause, began talking to them. She told them how much George had loved them—how much he loved this team. She told them that he had chosen Cornell because of them. She said, "This is a lesson to make sure you spend time with your friends, love your family, and look out for others. Tell your friends and family you love them." As she spoke she walked around and lovingly touched each young man on the head letting them know they were family, and they would get through this together. To this day, I don't know how she did it. Here, she and her husband had just lost their only son, and she was comforting us. She was dying on the inside, and the strength and love she had for all of us was superhuman. Looking back, we were all so young. I was 33 years old. Assistant coach Ben DeLuca was 29, assistant coach Patrick Dutton was 25, and our team was a bunch of

18-to-22-year-olds. We didn't know what to do. There was no playbook for something like this. We were shocked, scared, and hurting, and Mrs. Boiardi was our rock.

Years later, Mrs. Boiardi and I spoke about her talk to the team and I asked her how she found the strength to do it. She said that she knew our hearts were broken. When she looked at George's friends and teammates, she saw a bunch of young boys who needed to be comforted and loved, and she had to be there for them. They were all her sons.

The Hard Hat

Chapter 11

A Defining Moment

The coaches and the team weren't sure if we should cancel the rest of the season or not. Some of the guys wanted to play right away to take their minds off of everything while other guys didn't want to play on the field where they saw their friend and teammate die. We were all emotionally drained and uncertain about the future. We were scheduled to begin our spring break and travel to the University of North Carolina (UNC) to play them, but we decided to cancel the game. No one was prepared to play. We asked the players if they wanted to go home and spend spring break with their families or stay together, and everyone agreed that they wanted to do something as a team. So, we decided to travel to North Carolina anyway and spend some time there. We watched UNC play Duke at night. We went to the movies and played flag football, but we didn't play lacrosse. It was time to simply be together and get away from everything.

Then we traveled to Washington, DC, for George's funeral. I can still hear the song "On Eagle's Wings" playing. George's older sister, Elena, gave a very emotional eulogy. She talked about spending her junior year in college in Florence, Italy, far from George, who was at Cornell. She said, "Many are afraid of the dark, but [my sister] Caroline and I have no fear because

George was a great light. When George was near, you never saw your shadow . . . . One afternoon while in Florence, I walked through the rooms of the Bargello museum. I came upon a room that was filled with a great light; I was drawn into it. As I looked at the statues in the room, I came upon a niche and a statue of Saint George. I sat in front of it and wrote: '*You are young and beautiful and delicate, reflecting only peace. You watch over others in the soft light of the room. The darkness is gone. You may rest now, Saint George.*'"

The words she wrote on that day, several years before George's passing, spoke to all of our hearts about how we felt about George and the light that he brought to us. After the funeral, we traveled back to Ithaca for a memorial service where Mr. Boiardi spoke, and the last thing he said was, "I want to leave you with one thought: When a raindrop falls through still air toward a pool of water, it may momentarily catch the sunlight and refract a full spectrum of color. When the raindrop reaches the pool, it will disappear. But if the pool is perfectly calm, the energy transferred from that raindrop will continue in perfect concentric waves, spreading beyond our sight."

After the memorial service, we met as a team in the Hall of Fame room and talked about whether we were going to continue the season. Mr. and Mrs. Boiardi told us that if George could have his way, we would play. He would have wanted us to play and never give up. They gave us their blessing and the strength to move forward. So, we decided to continue the season, but we decided we were not going to play to win for George. We would play to honor the man and teammate he was. That didn't mean winning at all costs. We were going to play the way he had played the game and honor him through our actions and spirit. From that moment on, everyone focused on being a great teammate—not on winning—and we all changed. We became the ultimate team: selfless, committed, united, hardworking, passionate, and relentless. Never before had I been part of a team like that. It was a defining moment for us and for our program. If someone slacked off, we would look at the hard hat, which we had painted with George's number, 21. His presence never left us. Guys said that because George had never taken a play off, they wouldn't either. It was all about playing hard, playing tough, and having the integrity to do things the right way *all the time*—not part of the time—and staying committed to each other and George's legacy.

The irony of it all was that during a tragedy of that magnitude, the one person most of the team would have sought help from was George, and while he wasn't here physically, they were able to look to him for strength in a different way. We had been a team that lacked heart and George gave us his.

If you had a son, you wanted him to be like George. Mrs. Boiardi now had 42 sons, all striving to be like him. That's when everything changed.

Chapter 12

The Spirit of a Team

Our first game back was against Yale and it was scheduled for a Saturday afternoon. Our team wanted to wear a symbol of George to keep him close, so we decided to wear patches of the hard hat, complete with the number 21, on our jerseys. When our guys walked into the locker room and for the first time saw the game jerseys hanging in their lockers with the patches sewn on, it certainly stirred a lot of emotions.

As we began our pregame preparations, fog started to roll in and made it very difficult to see from one end of the field to the other. To this day, I have never seen anything like it. The cloud sat on the field and made it unplayable, so we moved the game to the following day. Many of the guys said it was a sign from George.

We played Yale on Sunday, which turned out to be a beautiful sunny Ithaca day. I will never forget the feeling coming out of the locker room. We placed a large picture of George in a Cornell Red uniform on a table to remind the team why we had chosen to be together on the field again. Each player walked past the framed photo of George with great emotion and took the field. It was a very somber experience, unlike your typical pregame feelings or rah-rah speech. Playing the game was like therapy for many of the players, giving them a chance to get back to something they loved, and doing it for a greater cause. We won the game 10–6.

Next, we traveled to Philadelphia and lost a close game to the University of Pennsylvania 10–8. They were a very good team that year and deserved credit for the win, but we played without much passion. The high from the Yale game had worn off and, as coaches, we could feel the emotional weight the kids were carrying. Looking back, I believe the lines regarding why we chose to play the season got blurry from time to time. Our emotions were difficult to manage and they started to wear our players down mentally. We were a fragile group, and you could see the tension between *playing* for George and *winning* for George increasing the pressure and making us lose clarity.

Prior to our next game, against Harvard, we had an impromptu meeting in the hotel after dinner to talk through a number of emotions. Through these conversations we were able to regain perspective as to *why* we were playing. The following day we came back from being several goals down to beat Harvard 10–9 in overtime, a result that provided the glimmer of hope we needed. The perspective gained from that pregame discussion carried us through an important stretch of the season that included both wins and losses.

After our exciting, improbable comeback against Harvard, we lost a tough game to Syracuse at home in the rain before playing Dartmouth and scoring with three seconds left to win 12–11. At that point, we had won almost every game against our Ivy League opponents in dramatic fashion, and now we were set to face our biggest rival, Princeton, on their home field.

It was the greatest game I have ever been a part of, given that George chose to come to Cornell instead of Princeton, whom we hadn't beaten in 10 years. Before the game, we sat in the locker room in a big circle, held hands, and talked about what George meant to each one of us. Each player spoke about the true meaning of being George's teammate and what this game would have meant to him. We had an amazing spirit, and that game changed the way we went through our pregame ritual forever.

It was a very competitive game and we went to overtime tied 11-11. JD Nelson, our face-off man, won the draw and we immediately called timeout. When we got back on the field, Justin Redd, one of our attackmen, was matched up with a short-stick defender, so he dodged from behind the goal, curled around past the goal line, immediately shot, and scored! We won 12–11. It was incredible. Everyone gathered around and hugged, but, as usual, we didn't have a crazy dogpile celebration. We were happy we won but knew it was just a game. It's not that we didn't care about winning or losing, but we felt like the consequences were nothing compared to losing George. We had a different spirit and a different perspective. The guys hung around for awhile after that game, celebrating with their families and enjoying the victory. It was extra special to see George's parents there. They had come to every game that season, to cheer us on. The fact that they did that still amazes me.

We didn't let up in our next game, against Brown, and somehow won that one 10–9, after scoring in the final seconds, to clinch a share of the Ivy League title. We were headed to the

The Spirit of a Team

NCAA tournament and our unpredictable, improbable, emotional season would continue. We played Hobart in the first round of the tournament, winning 11–5 and advancing to play Navy in the quarterfinals. Navy had one of the best teams in the country that year. We knew it would be challenging but we remembered why were playing and focused on George's values. We played Navy at home on Schoellkopf field, and as we ran into the stadium we saw a sea of red in the stands. Hundreds of people were wearing red Cornell shirts with the number 21 on them. It was very emotional. Just a few years before, the tragedy of 9/11 had occured, and the guys we were playing against would one day be fighting for our country. We respected them greatly for serving and honoring our country, but even so, we wanted to honor George with our play. It was a fiercely competitive game but, unfortunately for us, we lost 6–5.

Lacrosse is often referred to as *the healing game* by its Native American creators. With that loss to Navy, our season was over. I think that more disappointing than losing that game was the idea that our team wouldn't have the opportunity to continue to heal and bond each day in practice. We had overcome the greatest tragedy of our lives to accomplish more than we ever expected. Everyone was so proud of this resilient, selfless group of young men who gave everything they had to each other and our season. George's example became the spirit that inspired our team. He taught us the essence of being an honorable teammate and an authentic *team*.

Part Three

How to Be a Great Teammate

Chapter 13

George's House

 Having watched the 2007 team play in the NCAA semifinals and hearing Jeff talk about George and the 2004 season, I was struck by how clear it was that George impacted not only his team, but also Cornell's entire program. After all, many of the players on the 2007 team had never even met George, but they were still inspired by him.

The 2004 season was just the beginning of George's impact on the Cornell lacrosse program. Jeff told me that they had never reassigned his locker, which still has a picture of George and a #21 jersey inside. Guys see George's picture and are reminded of his spirit and presence every day. George lost his life playing the game he loved. How could the players who come after him not give their best effort? Everyone knew how hard he had played for the team, and they wanted to play well for him. As a result, Cornell's lacrosse team became a selfless and effort-driven program. Schoellkopf Field became known as "George's House." Before every home game, the team would say, "We have to protect George's house." Players tracked "Boiardi Stats," consisting of ground balls, hustle, and selfless plays, and those who played for the *team*—as opposed to personal glory—were recognized. "Boiardi Stats"

became part of the Cornell lacrosse vernacular and culture. If you were told to give a Boiardi-like effort, you knew you had to step up your drive and game. George's actions to organize his teammates to read to elementary school children eventually became an official program called the Big Red Readers program that still exists today. Upperclassmen told incoming freshmen about George, and the last class to play with him (2007 graduates) even made a video about George to share with future Cornell lacrosse players, which can be found on www.HardHat21.com.

George Boiardi: 21

Since learning about George and the 2004 season, I have followed the Cornell team and program very closely, and observed how they have climbed to a new level to become one of the top teams in the country. Since 2004, they have won the Ivy League title and made it to the NCAA tournament every year, except for 2012. They also made it to the NCAA Final Four in 2007, 2009, 2010, and 2013, and to the finals in 2009.

Anyone watching can feel that the Cornell team is driven by a bigger purpose, and now I understand the motivation behind it. They were no longer just playing lacrosse. They were playing for George, in George's House. They didn't focus solely on winning; they also focused on being great teammates. This didn't guarantee wins, but it guaranteed they would give their all to each other in the process.

Chapter 14

Learning from George

 Several years after my conversation with Jeff, I decided to attend the annual 21 Dinner in New York City. Hundreds of George's former teammates, friends, and family members gathered to support the Mario St. George Boiardi Foundation, which was founded by his friends and teammates. I didn't know exactly why I decided to attend, but felt I was supposed to be there.

The dinner was held in late January and a snowstorm hit the western Virginia area where I had a speaking engagement the day of the 21 Dinner. After the event that morning, I walked outside to heavy snowfall and found out that my flight to New York had been canceled. I had a choice. I could wait out the storm or find another way to get there. As fate would have it, the president of the company that had invited me to speak was also heading to New York. He pulled up in the back of a taxi headed to Washington, DC, where we could take a train to New York. I hopped in and we drove 182 miles, with our incredible driver, Samad, through a snowstorm on icy, unplowed roads, avoiding a few accidents along the way, to arrive just in time to make the last train to New York.

On the train, I thought a lot about George and wondered what was it about him that inspired his teammates so deeply.

I wondered if my friends would be affected the same way if I had died on the same field as George. Would hundreds be gathering for a dinner years later to support my foundation? Would a program have been transformed because of me? The honest answer was no. I wasn't the kind of teammate George was. I was a hard worker and I hustled, but at 18, 19, 20 years old, I was more concerned about myself than others. There were times I didn't give 100 percent. I didn't practice as much as I should have. I wasn't always consistent and didn't always lead by example. I wondered exactly what George had done, besides what Jeff shared, that made him such a great teammate.

After arriving in New York I took a cab to the 21 Dinner and arrived with a few hours left. I was thankful that I had made it. I didn't think I would, but I had to try because George would have. As I walked into the gathering, I realized that even though I had never met George, he was making me a better person. No wonder he had such an impact on the people he knew.

For the last few hours of the event, I sought out his teammates and friends and discovered more details about how he impacted the people he spent time with most. I learned what made George such a great teammate and, in doing so, I wanted to share those characteristics with others, like you. I can't change my past or change the kind of teammate I was, but by teaching you about George, I can help you create your future by helping you be a better teammate today. George's mom told me that while George didn't get a chance to fulfill his dream of being a teacher, he continues to teach others through the way he lived his life.

Although none of us will ever be Mario St. George Boiardi, we can learn from him and strive to be more like him. I believe that George was one of the greatest teammates to ever have lived, and serves as a model and teacher for all of us.

Chapter 15

21 Ways to Be a Great Teammate

A quote from Willard Straight above the fire place in Willard Straight Hall at Cornell University: *"Treat all women with chivalry • The respect of your fellows is worth more than applause • Understand and sympathize with those who are less fortunate than you are • Make up your own mind but respect the opinions of others • Don't think a thing right or wrong just because someone tells you so • Think it out yourself, guided by the advice of those whom you respect • Hold your head high and your mind open, you can always learn • Extracts from Willard Straight's letter to his son."*

1. Sweat More

Every one of George's teammates talked about his legendary effort, whether it was in the weight room or classroom, while running sprints or working on his stick skills, warming up or playing on the field. He always gave 100 percent in everything he did.

Mitch Belisle was a freshman when George was a senior, and what he remembers most about George was how much he would sweat during their weight-room sessions. He even joked that whenever George was his spotter when doing bench presses, George's sweat would drip on him. "We were paired up a lot during the fall workout sessions," Mitch said, "and all I remember is George's sweat dropping on me as I was trying to lift the weight. I can still remember the sight of George, his shirt drenched with sweat and it pouring from him . . . onto me. But George's sweat was indicative of how hard he worked. He was the hardest-working person I've ever met."

Scott Raasch remembers a night practice in February when it was so cold the turf was frozen over: "We were all doing our best to ignore how cold it was. After some pre-practice stick-work and warm-ups, Coach Tambroni called us into a huddle to announce the first drill of practice. In the huddle, I found myself standing directly behind George. I noticed that he was the only player visibly sweating through his pads and sweatshirt already, and the hair below the back of his helmet had formed into a mass of mini icicles. I was amazed and remember thinking, 'How in the world is George sweating like that already?' The rest of the night my goal was to push myself so that by the end of practice I'd be sweating like George was after *warm-ups*."

Lesson

As a team member, one of the things you control every day is your effort. When you work harder and sweat more, you bring out the best in yourself and your team.

2. Remember WD > WS

George was the ultimate definition of leading by example. He didn't ask for recognition, awards, or leadership positions. He just did things the right way and earned the respect and admiration of his teammates.

Andrew Collins, George's co-captain their senior year, said, "George lived by the motto: 'Well done is better than well said.' George didn't try to motivate you with his words. Instead he inspired you with his actions. As a result, I would always look at George and say to myself, he's trying to be as good as he can be so I need to strive to be the best I can be."

David "Moose" Mitchell, who was a freshman when George was a senior, said, "George did everything the right way. He was such a hardworking athlete and such a good, genuine person that you wanted to be like him. He was a good soul. You knew you could trust him, and because you trusted him, you followed him. Some leaders lead by charisma. George led by example."

Lesson

There's nothing wrong with words. Sometimes we need an inspiring message. Sometimes we need to be challenged and encouraged. Even George occasionally told the team to "pick it up" when he felt they weren't giving their best effort. But remember that, as a teammate, you speak most powerfully through your actions. Well said (WS) is important, but well done (WD) is always better, hence: WD > WS. Set the example in all that you do, so when you speak, people will listen because you have earned their respect by what you have communicated with your actions.

3. Choose to Be Humble and Hungry

Humility was a trait George's teammates in high school and college admired about him. (In fact, he would probably be mortified that a book like this was written about him.) It's that humility that inspires stories to be told. In addition to being humble, George was hungry with a burning desire to be his best and get better. George didn't settle for average. He had a hunger and a competitive spirit that drove him to take action and strive for excellence in all that he did. He didn't think he was a big deal, but his humility, hunger, and work ethic made him a big deal.

For example, after George's games in high school, his mom and dad would congratulate him, but instead of talking about his own performance, George wanted to talk about his team's effort instead. Mrs. Boiardi said, "If you look at team pictures, George was always in the background. He never sought the limelight. He never wanted recognition, accolades, or media attention."

George's friend Ian Rosenberger, whom he grew up with and also played lacrosse with at Cornell, said, "People heard about George because others talked about him, not because George talked about himself. People always talked about George but he never sought it or wanted the recognition. He actually deflected it. He was humble and never thought of himself as a big deal. He was an incredible athlete but wasn't cocky. He had the attitude of sometimes trying to just make the team. He always wanted to learn, improve, and get better."

Lesson

Humble and hungry are a powerful combination. The minute you think you have arrived at the door of greatness, it will get slammed in your face. The key to success is to be a lifelong learner who continuously works hard to improve. When you stay humble and hungry and focus on the process, you will love what the process produces.

4. Pursue Excellence

Because George was humble and hungry, he pursued excellence in everything he did. He didn't just *want* to be better. He *took action* to get better. He was always prepared, and if he didn't feel fully ready, he would prepare even more. In addition to being the last person to leave the locker room, he was also one of the first to arrive at the locker room for practice and games.

George's teammates reiterated what Jeff Tambroni told me about his pursuit of excellence. In the weight room he tried to get stronger. During running sessions he tried to get faster.

When they moved him to short stick from long stick, he spent countless hours trying to get better. Even though he ran the fastest 40-yard dash in the history of Cornell Athletics, he always tried to beat his time. He wasn't content with being the best. He wanted to be the best *he could be*. George didn't measure himself against others. His goal was a step above his previous best, and he pushed himself to get better. He took the same approach in the classroom, and spent hours studying and preparing for class and exams.

Lesson

Each day, it's important to wake up and strive to be better today than you were yesterday. Identify what you need to work on to get better and focus on improving each day. Don't settle for average. Instead, chase greatness. Realize that everyone wants to *do* what the great ones do but very few are willing to do what they *did* to become great. Be willing. Be humble and hungry. Pursue excellence. To help yourself and your team, implement the 1 percent rule, which says that a little more time, energy, effort, practice, focus, and care can bring big results. If you can push yourself to give just 1 percent more during each practice, each game, each film session, each class, each homework assignment, and each project, over time you will see big results.

5. Share Positive Contagious Energy

Not only were George's efforts and actions contagious, but his positive joyful spirit was as well. Even though he worked hard and was intense on the field, he was also joyful and positive in the locker room and in activities outside of lacrosse.

All of George's teammates said he was always positive and never said a mean thing about anyone. He had a genuine kindness that drew people to him, and when they did get close, he would always ask how they were doing. He wasn't just some guy on the team who worked hard. He was someone you respected and also liked being around. His smile lit up a room and people always felt better being around him.

He also loved to celebrate with his team and would often dance at parties until his clothes and sandals were covered with sweat. He had a love for life that was contagious to everyone who spent time with him. He listened to reggae with friends, played video games with fraternity brothers, rode his mountain bike around campus—he even sold ice cream from a truck on Nantucket Island the summer before his senior year with Ian Rosenberger and helped friends and teammates who were dealing with challenges. He had a group of close friends but he never formed cliques and he always shared positive energy with everyone on the team.

Lesson

As a team member, you not only control your effort but you also control your attitude. One of the most powerful things you can do to be a great teammate is to stay positive and share your positive energy with others. Research shows attitudes and emotions are contagious, and each day you can either infuse your team with positive energy or infect them with negative energy. You can be a germ or a big dose of vitamin C. When you share positive energy, you enhance the mood, morale, and performance of your team.

6. Don't Complain

Eleven years before George would set foot on the Cornell campus, I walked into my coach's office as a freshman and complained to him that I wasn't playing well. He walked me toward the office door and said, "Hey kid, we don't talk this game, we play it. Don't complain. Do it on the field." I went back to my dorm room, angry and upset, and decided I was going to show him on the field. Looking back, I realize he was teaching me the same lesson George shared with his teammates when the coaches moved him to short stick from long stick. Instead of complaining, George stayed positive and worked tirelessly to get better. Teammate Josh Heller told me that he never forgot how George handled the situation. He didn't complain once, when he had every right to complain. The coaches and even his best friends told me that he never said a word about it. Instead he focused on getting better and doing what the team needed him to do. Over time he would redefine the short-stick midfield position and become one of the best to have ever played the position.

Lesson

There are times when things don't go our way. There are situations that seem unfair. There are moments when we feel like we have a right to complain. But complaining causes us to focus on everything but being our best. When you work hard, stay positive, and do what the team needs, things always seem to work out. To be a great teammate, don't complain. Stay positive. You can't always control the events that happen to you, but you can control how you respond and, so often, this determines the outcome.

7. Do It for Your Team, Not for Applause

One of George's favorite quotes is carved above the fireplace in Willard Straight Hall at Cornell. It comes from a letter from Willard Straight to his son: "The respect of your fellows is worth more than applause." George's family and teammates told me that no one loved being part of a team more than George; everything he did was for the team, not for applause. He didn't love accolades or awards. He loved making his teams better. He loved helping them win. He loved making an impact, and did so by always putting the team first. Every one of George's teammates told me the same thing through different stories. They all said George would do whatever it took to make the team better.

Lesson

Great team members always put the team first. They work hard for the team. They develop themselves for the team. They serve the team. Their motto is whatever it takes to make the team better. They don't take credit; they give credit to the team. They have an ego and want to be great, but they give up their ego and serve the team, in order to be truly great.

It's not easy to put the team first, but if you want to be a great teammate like George, it's something you must work on.

In today's self-consumed world, you have to work as hard to be a great teammate as you do to be a great performer. In the end, your team doesn't care if you are a superstar. They care if you are a super teammate. And when you put the team first, you become a superhero in their eyes.

8. Show You Are Committed

George's teammates knew he put the team first because he demonstrated his commitment through his actions. One of George's teammates, Frankie Sands, told me a great story that showed how committed George was to his team: "During the off-season, Friday morning workouts were always the hardest. I think the coaching staff knew how excited everyone was to start enjoying the weekend on Thursday night, so they made it difficult for us. After a full lifting session we would go into the turf room for cardio training. One Friday, during George's junior year, we had to run six 300-yard timed runs to end the workout. Every player must finish in the given time for the lap to count. George was the fastest person on the team, and would consistently finish in the top three. During the fifth sprint George had an asthma attack and, as he finished the run, he couldn't catch his breath. Two or three players didn't finish within the time and we had to run the lap again. Coaches, captains, and our strength and conditioning coach all told George to sit this one out, but he had none of it. George viewed himself as a member of the team, and if everyone had to run, so did he. George was in a lot of pain and his face was eight shades of red. Today coaches definitely would have stopped practice to seek medical attention, but George made sure he finished under the time. Every player took motivation from him, and I wouldn't be surprised if our average time was faster on lap six than lap one."

Lesson

George was loved by his team because they knew how committed he was to them. If you want to be a great teammate, you can't just talk about how committed you are. You must demonstrate your commitment in all that you do. And always remember: If you want commitment, be committed.

9. Never Take a Play Off

One of the most defining characteristics about George was that he never took a play off. He never wavered or tried to skate by. He never took the easy road or let himself have a bad moment. He was consistent all the time in everything he did. His friend and teammate Tim Kirchner said, "After practice I would see George back at the fraternity house and most of the guys on the team wanted to chill on the couch and watch television but George would grab his books and start studying for an exam he had the next day. The same effort and consistency he showed on the field, he also demonstrated in school and every area of his life. He never took a play off, on or off the field. As a result, you always knew you could count on George."

Lesson

Most teammates are not consistent. They have good days and bad days. One day they are in a great mood, and the next day they are in a bad mood. One day they are saying nice things about a teammate, and the next they are badmouthing someone. One day, they give a great effort, but the next day they slack off. One day they yell and scream, but the next day they laugh and goof off. When you are inconsistent, your team doesn't know what to expect from you, and it makes it difficult for them to trust and count on you.

To be a great teammate, you want to be consistent in your attitude, effort, and actions. Like George, have a great attitude all the time so you can give your best in everything you do. Focus on becoming the best version of yourself every day. Don't change with the wind; instead, be like a strong-rooted tree that does not waver, regardless of what is happening around it. Be the kind of teammate everyone knows they can trust and count on.

10. Hold Yourself and Your Team Accountable

George wasn't just consistent; he was consistently great. He held himself accountable to the highest possible standards and held his teammates accountable as well. George set the example in all that he did and he expected others to follow that example. He didn't want them to follow him, but he wanted them to give their very best, like he did. His teammates said, most of the time, he held others accountable through his own actions.

For example, Chris Viola told me that as part of their Friday morning team training sessions they would start out by running a mile. George was always one of the first to finish, so he would go back to encourage the stragglers as they finished their final lap. Nothing said pick it up like George coming back to finish your lap with you after he had already finished his. Other times George would hold his team accountable with a powerful, quiet stare. They said he didn't speak often, but his eyes often told you what he was thinking. There were also a few times when he spoke to let everyone know he expected more from them. Whether it was "pick it up" or "come on, guys" or "let's go," George held his team accountable and wouldn't let them settle for less than their best. Tim DeBlois said, "George didn't hold you accountable like a police officer. He did it mostly through his example, and you wanted to do well because George did. He cared so much that he made you care."

David Mitchell never forgot the time George held him accountable. He said, "On the second to last rep of a 300-yard drill, I thought it was my last lap and was intent on finishing through the line. I'm sure I surprised a couple people by barreling through the finish, but George managed to grab my arm and slingshot me back into the drill for the final rep. There wasn't any yelling, in fact, not even a word was exchanged, but the message was received loud and clear that you aren't done until you are *done*. The whole thing didn't take more than three seconds, but that lesson will last me a lifetime."

Lesson

George's example is a simple and powerful one. To hold your team accountable, you first have to hold yourself accountable. When you expect the best of yourself, you can expect the best from your team, and when you expect the best from your team, they will rise up to meet your expectations. To be a great

59

teammate, you must hold your teammates accountable to the high standards of excellence your culture expects and demands.

11. Treat Everyone with Respect and Expect Everyone to Do the Same

George was also able to hold his team accountable because he had earned the moral authority by the way he treated others. All of his teammates with whom I spoke told me that he treated everyone with respect. Whether they were a freshman walk-on, an unpopular kid in high school, or a senior co-captain, George treated everyone with respect and he expected others to do the same.

Brigham Kiplinger said, "George didn't say much, but when he did, people listened. Once on the Landon [high school] hockey team, a senior who was sort of a jerk was giving a freshman a hard time by teasing him. George was only a sophomore and most of the young guys just stood by when that sort of mild hazing happened, but George told the senior to leave the freshman alone, and he did! George had the moral authority to say something because he was respected for his character, the way he treated people, and also for his work ethic—even as a younger player. He was also tough enough that the senior knew George would back up his words in defense of the freshman if he had to."

It was no surprise that George did the same thing in college. He treated everyone with respect, including the sandwich makers in the dining hall and the hotel workers when we traveled to games on the road. He respected everyone and, if someone wasn't showing respect, he would stand up for those who wouldn't stand up for themselves.

Lesson

To be a great teammate, it's important to respect and value each person for who they are, not what they do. When you respect everyone, as George did, everyone will respect you.

12. Give All and Take Nothing

George was a giver, not a taker. Justin Redd told me the thing he remembers most about George was: "He gave his all to the team but never took anything away from someone. He never made someone feel bad. He never called someone out in public. He never teased anyone. He never said anything mean about anyone. He gave you all his love, effort, respect, passion, commitment, and positive energy, and he never took anything positive from you."

Lesson

In a world where far too many energy vampires suck the energy out of the people around them, George is a great example of the impact you can have when you give all and take nothing. To be a great teammate, decide to be an energy fountain instead of an energy drain. Don't take anything positive away from anyone. Make your team better by giving the best within you to bring out the best in them. When you do, they'll never forget the way you made them feel.

13. Communicate

George didn't speak a lot in groups, but that didn't mean he wasn't a great communicator. His teammates all say George would let you know what he was thinking and feeling with his powerful eyes and smile. One stare said everything. One smile lit up a room. George also was a great listener and learned a lot about his teammates by asking questions and through one-on-one conversations. Many people like to communicate in groups, but George was more comfortable, talkative, and dynamic in one-on-one conversations, which is a key reason why he was such a great teammate.

I remember talking to NBA coach Doc Rivers and asking him the most important thing he does as a coach. He said, "I communicate to my team. Not just collectively but individually. I have to know where they are in order to lead them where they need to be." The same can be said for great teammates.

Lesson

To be a great teammate, it's essential to communicate with your team members collectively and individually. Communication builds trust. Trust generates commitment. Commitment fosters teamwork, and teamwork delivers results. Without communication, you can't build the trust and relationships necessary for great teamwork. Talking in team meetings and giving team speeches isn't enough. Great communication requires one-on-one conversations that help build relationships. In this spirit, I want to encourage you to make time to communicate with your teammates. Talk on the bus. Talk in the locker room. Eat with different team members each week. Don't just talk about the work at hand. Talk about your concerns and challenges, goals and dreams. When you are busy and stressed it's the last thing you want to do, but it's the most important thing you can do to build the kind of relationships that build great teams.

14. Connect

George did more than communicate. He also connected with his teammates. Communication begins the bond of building trust, but connection is where the bond is earned and strengthened. When you connect, you move past superficial conversations and communication; really get to know your teammates and develop a stronger bond with them. George created moments of connection (as you will read coming up) and in doing so he became the kind of teammate that impacted his team on a very deep and personal level.

Lesson

One of the biggest complaints I receive from coaches is that their teams aren't connected. They have a bunch of young men or women who usually focus on themselves, their own goals, and their own success. These young men and women usually have family members and friends telling them they should be playing more, scoring more, or getting more recognition. The message they receive from the world is that it's all about the individual, not the team. This creates a disconnect between personal and team goals, and it undermines shared success. I have found with the coaches and teams I have worked with, that when people focus on becoming a connected team, *me* dissolves into *we*. Bonds are strengthened. Relationships are developed and the team becomes much stronger. A connected team becomes a committed and powerful team.

As a teammate, one of the most important things you can do is connect with your teammates. After all, you can be the smartest person in the room, but if you don't connect with others, you will fail as a team member. Don't just communicate; connect. Get to really know your teammates. As you read about George and learn how he connected with his team, find your own moments of connection and you will be on your way to building a connected, committed, and powerful team.

15. Become a "Come with Me" Teammate

George's defensive coach, Ben DeLuca, said, "George was a *come with me* kind of leader and teammate. He never said, '*Do it because I said so.*' Instead, he would say, 'Come with me and let's work on our stick skills. Come with me and let's read to children. Come with me and let's run an extra lap together. Come with me and I'll give you a ride home. Come with me and let's get better.'"

David Coors said, "I came to Cornell as a walk-on trying to make the team and didn't know if I would fit in. I didn't participate in fall ball, and the freshman class, which included George, had developed a bond already. George somehow could sense how I felt and took me under his wing and got me involved in the group. But it wasn't just me. He was always looking after others to make them feel included. George also knew I needed to improve my stick skills, and since he was always working on his, he always invited me to practice with him. We spent a lot of time practicing our passing before and after practice and on weekends. He didn't just care about himself. He cared about helping me get better and I will always be thankful to him for that."

Lesson

If you want to be good, focus on making yourself better. If you want to be great, focus on making yourself and your team better. When you are with your team, identify who would benefit from your leadership, help, encouragement, and time and invite them to do something positive with you. Do this often, and over time you'll leave an incredible legacy.

16. Practice Selfless Compassion

David Coors's comments underscore an essential characteristic that made George a great teammate. He had incredible compassion and empathy for others and was always looking out for his teammates. He sensed who needed to be encouraged. He knew who felt like they didn't belong. He could tell who was feeling down after a long practice. He didn't focus on trying to make himself feel good. He always found ways to make his teammates feel better.

Chris Morea, who played on the same midfield with George for three years, said, "He had as strong a personal mission as I know. He genuinely put the needs of others in front of his own. It really was all about his family, teammates, friends, and community."

When I asked George's college girlfriend, Janna, what made him so special, she said, "It was his heart. Everything he did was from a kind, caring, and genuine place. When one of his teammates messed up, he didn't get mad at them; he wanted to help them. It was always about making someone or something better. When I would see him after practice, he always talked about what he could do to lead the team better. He wanted so badly to be a great captain for his team." Janna added, "One time I was visiting him during the summer in Nantucket and we were at the local supermarket. I turned around and George was gone. I found him a few minutes later in the parking lot helping an elderly woman put mulch in her car. That's who he was. He was Saint George."

Lesson

You can't be a great teammate if you are selfish. Great teammates like George are selfless. This doesn't mean they think less of themselves; it means they think of themselves less. They are more focused on others and think about how they can serve others. Always remember, you don't have to be great to serve, but you have to serve to be great.

17. Show You Care

George practiced selfless compassion and helped his teammates in a variety of ways, but he was most famous for giving rides home to the younger players who lived on North Campus, far away from the stadium and locker room. I lived on North Campus my freshman year and remember all too often walking back to my dorm room in the cold after a long practice. I wish George would have been my teammate when I played, because I could have used a ride.

Joe Boulukos was the recipient of one of George's rides and it's something he'll never forget. He said, "When I was a freshman I remember a really long practice that didn't go very well for me. I was feeling pretty down. I was assigned to take the laundry down to the equipment guys and thought I was the only person in the locker room. I cleaned up a few things, delivered the laundry, and prepared for a long walk back to North Campus. As I walked outside in the freezing cold, I saw a car sitting there like it was waiting for me. The window rolled down and I realized it was George. As I walked by the car he said, 'Do you want a ride?' Of course I hopped in, and on the way to North Campus, George, who was a junior at the time, asked how I was doing. I said I was doing fine but George knew otherwise. He then said, 'I know it was a long practice but I promise it's going to get better. You are doing great.' It was exactly the encouragement I needed at the time I needed it. As a freshman who was struggling, George, a guy I looked up to, showed he cared about me, and that meant everything."

Lesson

George embodied the truth that great teammates care more than others. Great teammates care more about their effort. They care more about their performance. They care more about how they are impacting the team. And, most of all, they care more about their teammates. George cared more about his teammates and they knew it, felt it, and will remember it forever.

To be a great teammate, it's important to show your teammates that you care about them. You may not drive people home from practice, but you can find your own unique way (I call this a caring trademark) that shows them you care. When you show your team you care about them, they will care about you. When you care, you will inspire others to care. When you care, you will build a team that cares, and a team that cares will accomplish amazing things together.

18. Be a Loyal Friend

When you are at a college party having a great time, the last thing you want to do is leave, but that's what George did one night to help Tim Kirchner. Tim said, "It was my twenty-first birthday and let's just say I had a little too much fun. I was about to leave by myself when George came running over to me and carried me home safely. I don't even think I could walk, so I guess George carried me most of the way. That's the kind of friend he was."

Ian Rosenberger and his sister were at a different party with George. Ian said, "I wanted to leave and go chase a girl I really liked but George wouldn't have any of it. He said, 'No, you have to take care of your sister.' George reminded me of what was most important and encouraged me to do the right thing. That's what friends do."

George was always there for his friends and, even when he made a mistake, he was as loyal as can be. Scott Raasch said, "During one of our first scrimmages against Loyola in 2004, I remember taking a huge hit as I turned around to pick up a ground ball off a face-off. Big hits were not that unusual in games, but the reason I remember this one so well is because right after, as I was trying to shake it off, I heard George say, 'Sorry, man.' It was probably the only time I can remember hearing someone apologize in the middle of a play. I'm not even sure George could've done anything to stop it from happening, but he blamed himself. Even in the locker room and at the parents' tailgate after the game, George wouldn't leave my side, and later that night he stopped by my room before I went to sleep to make sure I was okay. Before he left the room, I remember him turning around and saying, 'I promise you it will never happen again.'"

Lesson

A loyal friend and teammate is more precious than a diamond and more valuable than gold. They are very rare. My hope is that as you read this, you will increase the supply of loyal friends and teammates by deciding to be one today.

19. Love Your Team

When Mrs. Boiardi spoke to the team after George's death, she told them how much he loved them. Her words couldn't have been more powerful and appropriate. Underlying every story George's teammates shared with me was the love George had for his team. He loved his team and they knew it. George's sister Elena told me that he learned at an early age that family is a place where you love and are loved. The Boiardis had always been a very close-knit family that supported and loved one another, and when George went to Cornell, his team became his extended family and he loved and supported them the same way. Jeff Tambroni was the perfect coach for George, because family and love were a big part of the culture Jeff created and he considered the players to be part of his family. George found a college home where he was loved and loved others.

Lesson

Love truly is the greatest leadership principle and team-building strategy on the planet and if you don't have it, you can't share it. The truth is, if you don't love your team, you can never be a great teammate. Don't wait for your team to love you; first commit to loving them. I learned this lesson in my marriage and realized that the more I love my wife, the more I love my life. I'm not talking about the popular phrase *happy wife, happy life*. I'm talking about the fact that the more I focus on loving my wife without expecting anything in return, the more I love my life. It's not about what she does. It's about the love I give. As you focus on becoming a great teammate, learn from George and focus on loving your team. While many average players want their teammates to love them, you can become a great teammate by loving your team in spirit and action.

20. Sacrifice

If you love someone, you are willing to put their well-being and desires before your own. George loved his team so much that he was willing to give everything he had to inspire them. He gave his time, energy, sweat, and tears to become the best player possible for his team. He exposed his body to injury countless times by hitting bigger and stronger players and blocking shots. He suppressed his own desires to do whatever the team needed. He ignored the easy road to take the more difficult path of being a great leader, friend, and teammate.

Brigham Kiplinger said that it was the same love George had for his team that inspired him to apply to Teach For America to help Native American children in South Dakota. While many guys planned to graduate and seek their fortune in finance, George planned to serve others as a teacher. Tim DeBlois said, "When you combine all he did for his team with all he planned to do after graduation, you truly understand the magnitude of George's sacrifice."

As Tim talked to me, I couldn't help but wonder what was going through George's mind as he blocked the shot that March 17th night. No one believes he thought he was risking his life, but George knew the pain that would result and accepted that to help the team reach success. Although it hasn't been confirmed, many people believe George died from a condition called commotio cordis, that is, a sudden cardiac arrest caused by a blow to the chest. Because commotio cordis is often fatal, no one should block a shot with the chest, and every team should have a battery-powered AED (automatic electronic defibrillator) on the sideline.

Lesson

Please know I'm not saying you have to sacrifice your safety to be a great teammate. But you must be willing to give some of yourself for the greater good of the team. You have to be willing to sacrifice what you want for what the team needs. You have to decide to move from selfishness to selflessness. We live in a world where everyone wants to be great, but the truth is, only through service and sacrifice will anyone become great. This means you may have to play a different position than you are used to. You might dive for a loose ball in basketball or execute a sacrifice bunt in baseball. Perhaps instead of scoring, you can set a pick to help your teammate score. It means that sometimes you are the star and sometimes you help the star. George's last act was to jump in front of a shot; however, it was all the sacrifices he made for his team throughout his time with them that they talk about most, and I hope this will inspire you to sacrifice short-term pleasure and selfish desires for long-term respect, admiration, and impact.

21. Leave the Place Better than You Found It

Jeff Tambroni's message to his team was the same every year: *Leave the place better than you found it.* George's teammates said no one embodied this more than him. In fact, George had already lived by this philosophy before he ever met Jeff Tambroni or decided to go to Cornell. He was always the last to leave the locker room during his time at the Landon School, and he made sure he left it better than he found it. When he went to Cornell, he continued the practice. Every one of his teammates mentioned to me that George was always the last to leave the locker room. The image of George cleaning up while they said goodbye is imprinted in their minds. Some said that they now wished they had helped him more often. They were too busy running off to study or to eat or to see their girlfriends. They were off to live their busy lives. But George was focused on leaving the place better than he found it, and nothing can describe his time at Cornell better than Jeff Tambroni's mantra.

George left the Cornell lacrosse program better than he found it. His selfless leadership, warrior competitiveness, joyful spirit, undeniable loyalty, love, compassion, and heart made his team and Cornell lacrosse better because of the way he led and lived. Consider the team's magical season in 2004 and their return to prominence thereafter. George had made a great impact.

Nothing describes George's impact better than the words of one of the greatest lacrosse players in history, Rob Pannell, who graduated from Cornell in 2013. As you read Rob's words in the next chapter, realize that he never even met George. That's how dedicated George was to leaving the place better than he found it.

Chapter 16

21: A Way of Life

Narrated by Rob Pannell

When working out, instead of doing 15 or 20 reps, I do 21. Instead of running 15- or 20-second sprints, I run 21-second sprints. Instead of running on the treadmill for 15 minutes, I run for 15 minutes and 21 seconds. Every time I have the opportunity to see the number 21, I take it. Every time I see the number 21, I think of George Boiardi. For me, 21 is not a number—it's a way of life.

If I could meet two people in the world, I would choose George Boiardi and Eamon McEneaney (who wore number 10 on his jersey). Eamon was another Cornell lacrosse legend; he died in the 9/11 attacks on the World Trade Center. Believe it or not, growing up I wore three numbers in sports: 10, 21, and 3. The number 3, my number at Cornell, doesn't belong in the same sentence as 10 and 21, but I could not have been in a more fitting situation than playing for the Cornell lacrosse program, where those numbers carry such enormous weight and tremendous honor. Unfortunately, I never met George, but I feel as if he has been a teammate and leader to me during my five years at Cornell and is now a friend helping me through my everyday life.

Rarely does a day go by when I don't see the clock strike 10:21. That's no coincidence; it's just George and Eamon checking in. I will never forget scoring to put Cornell up 1–0 in the 2013 semifinal against Duke. The game clock stopped and read 10:21. I looked at our sideline and pointed to the clock. Everyone was looking at me, yelling and thinking I was crazy, but they soon realized I was trying to say that George was there with us, just as he is every other day. Without 21, Cornell Lacrosse is not Cornell Lacrosse, and I'm not the player and, more importantly, the person who I am today. George didn't help us beat Duke that day, because that wasn't what George was all about—but he had made us better people and teammates, and that carried us through a successful season.

According to the record books, I hold the Cornell Lacrosse record for most assists. The real truth is that George Boiardi does. George has gotten an assist for every single practice, weight session, film session, ground ball, goal assist, win, and on and on, since his freshman year at Cornell—and he still does, because without his number 21, none of those experiences would have been the same. The emotion, the effort, the intensity, the focus, the love made all the difference. The number 21 is a way of life. Selfless, loving, caring, tireless, humble, dedicated. These words define George Boiardi. George Boiardi defines Cornell Lacrosse.

Part Four

Legacy

Chapter 17

Great Teammates Impact You Forever

In the years since learning about George from Jeff Tambroni and his teammates, I have thought about him often. I had the honor of speaking at the 21 Dinner a few years ago and have learned even more details about his life. I have often shared stories about him when speaking to student-athletes and, as a parent, I find myself telling my children stories about George and encouraging them to follow his example as a leader and teammate. I have also followed, via social media, all the various events that have been created to further George's legacy and mission, including the 21 Run, the Boiardi Open golf tournament, Team 21, and the Capital Lacrosse Invitational. It's been amazing to see how George continues to live on more powerfully and influentially than ever as his friends and teammates remember him, and other people, like me, learn his story and become inspired by him.

When I read that George was going to be inducted into the Cornell University Athletic Hall of Fame, 10 years after his death, I immediately marked the date on my calendar and made plans to attend the dinner.

On my flight to Ithaca, I thought of all the events that George's teammates created to carry on his legacy, and it occurred to me that those teammates won't let him be forgotten. They can't. He made too big an impact on their lives to let him disappear. Then, I looked at myself and realized I couldn't forget about George, either. His life, lessons, and message were too powerful for me to forget and too important not to share with others.

As I thought about the impact George had on his team and the Cornell lacrosse program, I realized that great leaders and teammates don't just impact you today; they impact you for the rest of your life. I wondered how George had impacted his teammates and coaches 10 years later. Did he impact their work, careers, relationships, families? Did anyone name their kids George?

When I walked into the event, I was excited to see that a lot of his teammates, friends, and coaches were there to honor him. They were a little older, a little heavier, a little wiser, more reflective, and willing to share how much they missed their dear friend and the impact he continued to make in their lives.

Chapter 18

Live and Lead Like George

 Andrew Collins said an interesting thing about life is that, when someone dies, his or her memory usually fizzles over time, but just as George never wavered, his impact hasn't, either. When I asked Andrew why, he said, "Because George never asked for it. It's who he was. He was larger than life without trying to be larger than life. To this day, I often ask myself, 'Is this how George would have lived his life?' I can't be George but I can strive to be like him. Remembering him makes me better. Every day I take his lessons and apply them to my life as a husband and new father. In my role as a sales manager, I never ask my team to do things I wouldn't do. Instead of telling them, I remember George's example, and I get in there and do the work and show them how it's done."

Kyle Georgalas, who is now an assistant coach for the Army lacrosse team, said, "George made me a better teammate and now he makes me a better coach. I have more empathy and strive to serve my team. I go to the library to meet with players during the off-season instead of making them come to my office. I focus more on developing relationships with my players to help them be their best."

George's coach, Ben DeLuca, who is now an assistant for the Duke University lacrosse team, said, "Two events in my life have transformed my coaching philosophy: 9/11 and George's passing. Losing George on the field that day taught me perspective and how to focus on relationships. I now let my team know I love them. I drive them to be their best, but let them know I care about them. To this day, I compare every player to George, and the biggest compliment I can give a young man is that he reminds me of George and hustles like he did."

When I asked Mitch Belisle what he thinks about when he remembers George, he said, "I think about the huge impact he had on me in such a short amount of time. He was alive for only 22 years and made a bigger impact than most people who live 80 years. To this day, I do 21 reps instead of 20. I give more effort and work harder because of George. I run a lacrosse company and still play pro lacrosse and have the honor of wearing 21 for my team. And one of the greatest honors of my life was wearing number 21 for Team USA this summer at the World Games."

David Coors still remembers the sight of George sitting in his room on the couch, eating a sub, watching television. He said, "Our rooms shared a common area and since George was president of the fraternity, he had a master key. When I would come back from class there was George, hanging out in my room. He was never about appearances, and clothes weren't a big deal to him, so he would often borrow my dress shirts and socks. Because it was George and he was the kind of person who would give the shirt off his back to someone in need, it never seemed to bother me. He was such a free spirit and I

82

loved him. To this day I get up and go surfing in Sydney, Australia, at 5:30 a.m. before work to get the most out of life. When friends ask my wife and I to go out, we always say yes. When I get an invite, I say yes. Life is short and I want to make the most of it."

Justin Redd said, "I think about him every day. I think about how unfair it is that he didn't get to live on—how unfair it is that people didn't get to meet him and know him. I think about all the kids that didn't get to be taught by him and the family he didn't get to have. I realize how lucky I am to have those things, and more to look forward to. When something doesn't go right in my life and I come up short, one of the first things I think is, 'George would never have done that.' He's still a guide on how to live. George never took the easy road and neither will I."

Billy Fort said, "I don't think about George when things are going great. I don't know why, but I think about him when things aren't going great. I think that's when I look to him for strength to get through whatever adversity I'm facing. George was always helping his friends and he continues to help me now to live and lead like him."

When I asked Janna, George's college girlfriend, how he has impacted her life 10 years later, she broke down in tears and said, "When I met George I had been through a lot, and yet George loved me with my flaws and all. George was so loving, so kind, and so thoughtful, he taught me I could love again. He helped me become the woman I am today."

Tim DeBlois was on the field next to George when he died. He said, "I think about all the people George would have touched if he had lived, and I feel a duty to touch

Live and Lead Like George

people's lives and impact others. I wear a bracelet on my wrist with George's number on it and am constantly asking myself if I can do more. I don't ask in a negative way. George never made you want to do more out of obligation. He made you want to do more to be your very best and, to this day, he makes me want to be my best as a son, brother, soon-to-be husband, and, hopefully, a father."

Nii Amaah Ofosu-Amaah, who went to high school with George, has since become great friends with George's college teammates. He said, "I think about George every day. Through 10 years of joy, blood, sweat, and tears at Landon together, he is part of who I am and who I have become. I remember fondly being cornered in a bar at home in DC over the holidays our senior year of college and getting grilled by George about my new girlfriend (now wife) and pursuits post-college. With all the distractions we have today, it's a special feeling to have 100 percent of someone's attention. Remembering how immersed George was in each of our interactions (and how rare and good that felt), I attempt to be fully absorbed in the moments I have with my friends and family: 100 percent effort, 100 percent attention, just like George always [gave to] everyone."

Tim Kirchner, who helps run the Mario St. George Boiardi Foundation with several of George's other teammates and friends, said, "From my decision to halt a New York job search and return home to San Francisco in May of 2004, to my coaching lacrosse that spring and thereby landing the day job I have held for the past nine years, my trajectory has George's fingerprints all over it. And just as George led me to my job, he also led me away from it, serving as a reminder to make time for the more important things when my nephew was born, my parents were sick, or my friends needed help, and to have the courage to step away when I felt I could do more good elsewhere. And now I feel fortunate to be logging many hours with George, which is how I think about my work leading his foundation."

Chapter 19

What Would George Do?

 Ian Rosenberger said, "If I ever have a son, I want him to be just like George, and each day I strive to be the kind of man George would be proud of." It's a sentiment many of his teammates and friends shared with me. Scott Raasch said, "There's one item I've always had on my desk at work during the past 10 years. Mr. and Mrs. Boiardi gave each senior on our team a paperweight for graduation with the phrase "Well Done Is Better than Well Said" engraved on it—the same one George had growing up. It's a daily reminder to always try and be more like George, and let good deeds and hard work speak for themselves. I also took one of the Boiardi Foundation wristbands and wrapped it around the paperweight. It's remarkable how many of George's friends from Landon and Cornell have come together over the years to work on his foundation and continue his mission and legacy."

Josh Heller said, "My father and George are the two biggest influences in my life. It's amazing that, as a college kid, he had that kind of influence. As you get older and achieve some success, you find yourself around all types of people and remember that George treated all of them, no matter who they are, with respect. I strive to do the same."

Brigham Kiplinger traveled in the summer of 2004 to the reservation where George was hoping to teach, just to experience where George would have spent his time. "To this day I think about him all the time. He still drives me. He is the paragon that I want to be. George is the reason why I have stayed in teaching. I am now doing the work for both of us. Even though his life was cut short, he taught so many of us. George was a teacher and he still is. I often think about what George would do and that's how I live my life."

Michael Riordan said, "Ten years after Mrs. Boiardi presented each Cornell lacrosse player with the St. George pendant, it still hangs from my neck. Since his passing, I can probably count on my hands the number of days that George has not entered my mind. When apathy finds me in the gym, my memory of George's competitive fire in the weight room motivates me to match his intensity. When fatigue finds me at the library, George's unyielding persistence in his most challenging classes reminds me not to give up. When irritability finds me in the hospital, I remember George's genuine kindness to everyone he encountered. George became the person I emulated when searching for a career. I wanted a job where I could help people. I chose medicine. Hopefully, George would be happy with my choice."

Joe Boulukos credits George not only for giving him rides home from practice, but also for introducing him to his wife. He met his wife, Nicole, at a 21 Dinner several years ago and they are expecting a baby. Joe and Nicole are leaning toward the name George if the child's a boy. Joe said he thinks about George all the time and asks himself often: "Am I being a good person? Am I doing the right things? Am I helping others?"

Chapter 20

A Hall of Fame Legacy

 When I asked George's teammates if they had died on the field that day instead of George would there have been the same response and impact, every one of them said emphatically, "No, definitely not." I told them I felt the same way about myself as a teammate. Yet on this day, many of them came from different areas of the country and the world to be at George's Hall of Fame induction. David Coors flew to Ithaca from Australia, and was flying right back after the event. Chris Viola came for the induction and afterward had to turn around and head right back to the restaurants he owns in New York City. Tim Kirchner flew in from San Francisco. Others gave up their weekends and time with family, friends, and kids to be there. They may not have been the kind of teammates George was in college, but 10 years later they were being selfless, serving, and sacrificing—10 years later he was still making them better.

That night Jeff Tambroni delivered an inspirational, emotional, tear-jerking speech about George. He had to stop numerous times to gather himself and wipe the tears from his eyes, face, and notes. It was one of the most meaningful and powerful speeches I have ever heard, and there wasn't a dry eye in the room. Jeff is no longer the lacrosse coach at

Cornell. He now coaches the men's lacrosse team at Penn State University. He didn't take the hard hat with him, but he takes George's spirit, example, and inspiration wherever he goes. He will always be George's coach and George will always be a part of him.

As Jeff and I left the event and walked outside to our cars, I asked him where he was staying. It was midnight and, since he was leaving, I figured, like me, he was staying at a hotel near campus. Jeff said, "Actually I'm driving to Philadelphia right now. There's a recruiting tournament in the Philly area and I have to be at the fields at 8 a.m. I'll drive as far as I can and get a few hours sleep, then get to where I need to be in the morning." I did the math: four to five hours of driving meant two to three hours of sleep. Not to mention that Jeff had driven to Cornell that day to give his speech. I was blown away. I couldn't believe he had sacrificed like that, but Jeff had to be there. So did David Coors, Tim Kirchner, Ben DeLuca, and so many of George's teammates. They wouldn't have missed it. George would have done the same.

21 Exercises to Build a Great Team

 When I finished writing Chapter 20, I thought I was finished with the book, but then I realized I had to write one more for George. George always gave a little extra and so should I; 20 chapters would have been good but 21 makes the book that much better.

I've learned from George that 21 is not a beginning or an end, but a journey to being your best and bringing out the best in others. George was all about making his team better, so it was fitting that, as I contemplated what to write on these last pages, I was inspired to fill this last chapter with ideas to make your team stronger and better.

You see, I believe George was here on earth for a reason: to inspire us to be better people and teammates. George's parents, Mario and Deborah; his sisters, Elena and Caroline; and his friends and teammates continue to get signs from George, and this continues to give them strength and hope. And as I wrote this book, I kept seeing 21 on my phone, email, Twitter notifications—everywhere. I am convinced that everything in my past has brought me to this moment to share George's story to help you and your team. The fact that you're reading this book is not an accident. My hope is that you will share this book with your team, family, and friends, and then implement some of the exercises in this chapter. I believe this will help you become the best team possible and, in the process, you'll be sharing George's story, lessons, inspiration, and purpose with others.

As you utilize this book and share it with others, you can feel good knowing that 100 percent of my royalties will be donated to the Mario St. George Boiardi Foundation to continue George's mission and legacy. George gave his all to his team and the least I can do is give my all to him and your team. In this spirit, here are 21 exercises to build a great team.

1. Talk about the book as a team and ask each team member what they thought about the book. Ask what they learned, what inspired them, and what they took away from the book.

2. Have each person identify and share several characteristics George had that are also prevalent on the team. Write all the answers on a whiteboard and see which ones come up the most. Talk about these characteristics and identify ways you can make them even stronger.

3. Have each person identify and share characteristics George had that are missing most from the team. Write all the answers on a whiteboard and see which ones come up the most. Talk about these characteristics as a team and identify ways you can develop them with your team.

4. Have each team member choose their three favorite *ways to be a great teammate* and focus on putting them into action for the year.

5. Have each team member identify and share where they fall short as a team member. Allow people to be open, honest, and transparent. Don't judge. Use this as an opportunity to connect and grow.

6. Have your teammates evaluate each other and share which of George's characteristics they possess and which characteristics they are lacking and need to work on. If a teammate has the mindset "I'm open. Make me better," and they are willing to listen and change, they will become a much better teammate and you will become a much better team.

   A word of caution: This activity is a little more challenging and can backfire without the right approach; however, if done right, it will make you a much more powerful and connected team.

7. Divide your team into small groups of two or three people. Have each group present one or two of the 21 ways to be a great teammate from Chapter 15 to the rest of the team. They can teach through a lesson, video, song, poem, or skit. Be as creative as you want. This helps bring the lesson to life.

8. Create a hard hat with your chosen colors or consider establishing a different symbol that will help you build your team culture with the characteristics that you want.

9. Share the three things that every teammate can control to be a great teammate: (1) effort, (2) attitude, and (3) actions. Then ask each team member to identify one habit for each thing they control that will make them a better teammate.

10. Share this statement with your team: *Team beats talent when talent isn't a team*. Then ask your team what this means to them and how you can become a better team.

11. Have each team member share a defining moment in their life. You'll learn things you never knew before. Immediately, you will know your team members a whole lot better and feel more connected to them.

12. Hero, highlight, hardship: With this exercise have each person name one of their heroes and why they admire that person. Then, have them share a positive highlight and a hardship from their past. Their answers will give you a lot of insight into your team members' motivations and perspectives. Note: For this to work, it must be understood that what is said in the room stays in the room. You must create a space (one leader I worked with called the meeting room "the safe place") where people feel comfortable being honest and vulnerable.

13. Get on the Energy Bus together. Visit www.theenergybus .com and print out free bus tickets to hand out to your team. On the backs of the tickets, have each person write one commitment they are making to the team and have them hand in the bus ticket, letting the team know they are buying in and on the bus.

14. Fuel up the tanks. Give each player a manila envelope with a picture of a bus and their name on it. The envelopes represent their energy bus gas tanks and should be placed on a table in the locker room. Give index cards to each person so they can write something positive about a teammate and place the card (positive

The Hard Hat

fuel) in their teammates' manila envelope (energy bus tank). After practices and games, encourage your team to write positive comments and fill their teammates' energy bus tanks with positive energy. The exercise creates more positive interactions and generates appreciation and encouragement that fuels the team throughout the year.

15. Play "If You Really Knew Me." Start by filling in the blank in this statement: "If you really knew me, you would know _____ about me." I learned this exercise from my friend and author Mike Robbins and, even though it forces people to be vulnerable, it is one of the most powerful exercises a team can do. I recently took a leadership team through this exercise and at first they shared very shallow comments like "If you really knew me, you would know that I'm very generous and wonderful." But after challenging them to go deeper, then backing it up by sharing something vulnerable about myself, they started sharing meaningful stories and feelings that connected the team in a deep and powerful way.

16. Make it a point to eat with different team members each week. The more time you spend with different team members, the more connected you become.

17. Have your team make up a list of 20 questions. While traveling, before getting on your phones and firing up the social media, get team members to ask and answer the 20 questions about each other. This will help you get to know your team members and become more connected.

21 Exercises to Build a Great Team

18. Talk about the ways George showed he cared, then explain how cleaning the locker room and driving freshmen home are examples of a caring trademark (something memorable you do to show people you care about them). Explain the concept of a caring trademark to your team. Then have each team member decide what their caring trademark will be and when and how they will put it into action.

19. Have each team member choose one word that will help drive them to be the best team member they can be. You may choose a word such as: connect, commit, serve, give, help, care, love, tough, relentless, excellence, and so on. Each person should choose a word that is the right fit for them. Visit www.Getoneword.com for more ideas. You can then put all the words on your hard hat or other team symbol.

20. Talk about the 1 percent rule: A little more time, with a little more energy, effort, focus, and care equals big results. Have each member identify where they need to invest more time, energy, effort, and focus. If each team member invests 1 percent more each day, over time the team will create big results.

21. Have each team member create and share a legacy statement that includes the kind of impact they want to have on their team. How do you want to be remembered? What do you want others to say about you after you have moved on from the team? Knowing how you want to be remembered helps you decide how to live and lead today.

The Big Red

by the Boiardi Family

During the 11 years since the Cornell University men's lacrosse season of 2004, George has been in the hearts and minds of his family and friends on a daily basis. The healing process resulting from the wrenching loss of him continues. The Big Red spirit that enveloped us all when we became part of the Cornell family, however, has lifted us up and kept us moving forward.

Many young men have their lives cut tragically short. Their families bear their loss and their friends help to console them. We keep these families in our hearts and prayers. We feel blessed that we have had the support of the Big Red family to console us. It has been remarkable to us how constant and ardent George's teammates, friends, and Cornell University have been in their commitment to keep the memory of George alive.

During a period of their lives when they have been starting careers and families, his teammates and friends have spent countless, precious hours raising funds for causes that George would have also been committed to. They established the Mario St. George Boiardi Foundation to raise and donate funds to charitable causes. Initially all of the proceeds from annual winter gatherings at the 21 Dinner in New York City went to support the newly formed Teach For America—South Dakota. The 21 Run over the Cornell University Plantations roads, where George loved to ride his long skateboard, follows each scheduled men's lacrosse season and lends support to the Family Reading Partnership of Ithaca. The 21 Run West has been held in San Francisco's Golden Gate Park. There have been charity golf tournaments in the Washington, DC, area. For the last three years, the Foundation has organized the Capitol Lacrosse Invitational "fall ball" lacrosse tournament for Division One teams at the Landon School in Bethesda, Maryland, where George was a student from third grade through high school. Currently the proceeds from all these activities support the mission of the Mario St. George Boiardi Foundation: "to empower youth through academics and athletics."

Perhaps most dear to George of all these activities might be the culmination of a dream he shared with David Coors: to play with their teammates in the Vail Lacrosse Shootout summer tournament. David, his family, friends, and Cornell teammates made this dream come true by playing as Team 21 for years and winning the tournament on July 6, 2008.

Cornell University posthumously granted George his degree and established an award in his name for athletes in the Senior Class. The "Wall of Records" in the Friedman Strength and Conditioning Center, where he sweated with his teammates, was named in his honor. The University Athletic Department placed a commemorative plaque, dedicated by his teammates, outside the men's lacrosse locker room at

Schoellkopf Field, next to plaques memorializing #10 Eamon McEneaney '77 and #42 Jay Gallagher. Last fall the Athletic Department placed his name in the Athletic Hall of Fame. His locker remains his and his photograph is in the locker room next to one of Eamon. The men's lacrosse team continues to refer to Schoellkopf Field as "George's House" and they continue to organize and participate in the 21 Run.

George would be humbled by these tributes and they continue to amaze us, but in the context of the Big Red family they are not surprising. When we attended the team dinner in the fall of 2003, we listened to Coach Tambroni introduce the freshmen and their parents. Deborah remembers thinking that "they don't know what a great experience they will have as part of this family." It wasn't just the players and coaches, but the parents, siblings, aunts, uncles, cousins, and friends who were part of the Big Red family.

The five-hour drive from Washington, DC, through the Endless Mountains of Pennsylvania was never a bother. We looked forward to the end of the trip when we would gather with the Big Red family outside Schoellkopf Field or in the Hall of Fame Room where we waited with great excitement to watch the game and then to see our sons and their teammates. The welcome we received was always warm and genuine. Everyone shared the Big Red spirit. The games were intense, but the gatherings afterwards were joyous. We did have fun!

Lesson:

Whether in athletics or life, it's not all about winning, but everything about the opportunity to PLAY THE GAME.

Afterword

George

From the time he first jumped out of his crib at his sister's urging, George took joy in the gift of his physical abilities. He was always an outdoors kid: running, jumping, riding bikes, sledding, skating, or just swinging on the big rope swing hung from the gigantic Tulip Poplar tree near our house. When he grew older, he excelled in sports that required agility and speed. He took joy in bounding over turf on his nimble feet, skimming over ice on razor-sharp blades, floating through the air in a dive or flight from a mountain. What appeared so natural and effortless for him were gifts that he joyously celebrated every day. As much as anything else, his agility and speed carried him to Schoellkopf Field his last evening. Once again he was celebrating his gifts, playing lacrosse with his teammates. When he passed away, we know he had joy in his heart. For that we always give thanks.

Lesson

Be joyful and CELEBRATE YOUR GIFTS.

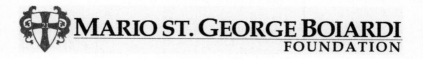

MARIO ST. GEORGE BOIARDI
FOUNDATION

F or more information about the Mario St. George Boiardi
Foundation and to support the mission, visit:

boiardifoundation.org/

theboiardifoundation@gmail.com

Photos

George

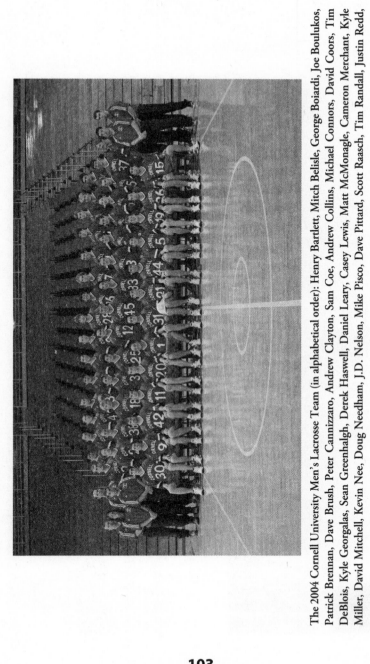

The 2004 Cornell University Men's Lacrosse Team (in alphabetical order): Henry Bartlett, Mitch Belisle, George Boiardi, Joe Boulukos, Patrick Brennan, Dave Brush, Peter Cannizzaro, Andrew Clayton, Sam Coe, Andrew Collins, Michael Connors, David Coors, Tim DeBlois, Kyle Georgalas, Sean Greenhalgh, Derek Haswell, Daniel Leary, Casey Lewis, Matt McMonagle, Cameron Merchant, Kyle Miller, David Mitchell, Kevin Nee, Doug Needham, J.D. Nelson, Mike Pisco, Dave Pittard, Scott Raasch, Tim Randall, Justin Redd,

103

Photos

#21 retired April 2004

2004 team gathers at Schoellkopf Field

104

Photos

Fans watch Cornell play Navy in 2004

Tommy Johnson (artist)

105

Photos

George's locker

Mitch Belisle, USA 21

Max Siebald, Rob Pannell, Jeff Tambroni, Ben DeLuca, Mitch Belisle

107

Photos

Chief Red Cloud's monument at Pine Ridge, South Dakota, where George
wanted to teach with Teach For America

The 21 Run at the Cornell University Plantations

108

Photos

WD > WS paperweight

St. George pendant

109

Photos

Become A Great Teammate

Visit www.HardHat21.com to:

- Print posters with memorable quotes from the book.
- Share *The Hard Hat*'s practical principles with your organization and team.
- Learn how other teams have utilized the Hard Hat principles.
- Watch videos and hear from George's teammates in their own words.
- Get the Hard Hat team building action plan.

Build Your Best Team

If you are interested in bringing *The Hard Hat*'s inspiring message to your leaders, organization, and/or team, contact the Jon Gordon Companies at:

Phone: (904) 285-6842

E-mail: info@jongordon.com

Online: JonGordon.com

Twitter: @jongordon11

Facebook: Facebook.com/JonGordonpage

Instagram: JonGordon11

Sign up for Jon Gordon's weekly e-newsletter at JonGordon.com.

To purchase bulk copies of *The Hard Hat* at a discount for large groups or your organization, please contact your favorite bookseller or Wiley's Special Sales group at specialsales@wiley.com or (800) 762-2974.

Other Books by Jon Gordon

The Energy Bus

A man whose life and career are in shambles learns from a unique bus driver and set of passengers how to overcome adversity. Enjoy an enlightening ride of positive energy that is improving the way leaders lead, employees work, and teams function.

www.TheEnergyBus.com

The No Complaining Rule

Follow a VP of Human Resources who must save herself and her company from ruin, and discover proven principles and an actionable plan to win the battle against individual and organizational negativity.

www.NoComplainingRule.com

Training Camp

This inspirational story about a small guy with a big heart, and a special coach who guides him on a quest for excellence, reveals the eleven winning habits that separate the best individuals and teams from the rest.

www.TrainingCamp11.com

The Shark and the Goldfish

Delightfully illustrated, this quick read is packed with tips and strategies on how to respond to challenges beyond your control in order to thrive during waves of change.

www.SharkandGoldfish.com

Soup

The newly appointed CEO of a popular soup company is brought in to reinvigorate the brand and bring success back to a company that has fallen on hard times. Through her journey, discover the key ingredients to unite, engage, and inspire teams to create a culture of greatness.

www.Soup11.com

The Seed

Go on a quest for the meaning and passion behind work with Josh, an up-and-comer at his company who is disenchanted with his job. Through Josh's cross-country journey, you'll find surprising new sources of wisdom and inspiration in your own business and life.

www.Seed11.com

One Word

One Word is a simple concept that delivers powerful life change! This quick read will inspire you to simplify your life and work by focusing on just one word for this year. *One Word* creates clarity, power, passion, and life-change. When you find your word, live it, and share it, your life will become more rewarding and exciting than ever.

www.getoneword.com

The Positive Dog

We all have two dogs inside of us. One dog is positive, happy, optimistic, and hopeful. The other dog is negative, mad, pessimistic, and fearful. These two dogs often fight inside us, but guess who wins? The one you feed the most. *The Positive Dog* is an inspiring story that not only reveals the strategies and benefits of being positive, but also an essential truth: being positive doesn't just make you better; it makes everyone around you better.

www.feedthepositivedog.com

The Carpenter

The Carpenter is Jon Gordon's most inspiring book yet—filled with powerful lessons and success strategies. Michael wakes up in the hospital with a bandage on his head and fear in his heart after collapsing during a morning jog. When Michael finds out the man who saved his life is a carpenter, he visits him and quickly learns that he is more than just a carpenter; he is also a builder of lives, careers, people, and teams. In this journey, you will learn timeless principles to help you stand out, excel, and make an impact on people and the world.

www.carpenter11.com

You Win in the Locker Room First

Based on the extraordinary experiences of NFL Coach Mike Smith and leadership expert Jon Gordon, *You Win in the Locker Room First* offers a rare, behind-the-scenes look at one of the most pressure-packed leadership jobs on the planet, and what leaders can learn from these experiences in order to build their own winning teams.

www.wininthelockerroom.com

Life Word

Life Word reveals a simple, powerful tool to help you identify the word that will inspire you to live your best life while leaving your greatest legacy. In the process, you'll discover your *why*, which will help show you how to live with a renewed sense of power, purpose, and passion.

www.getoneword.com/lifeword

The Power of Positive Leadership

The Power of Positive Leadership is your personal coach for becoming the leader your people deserve. Jon Gordon gathers insights from his bestselling fables to bring you the definitive guide to positive leadership. Difficult times call for leaders who are up for the challenge. Results are the byproduct of your culture, teamwork, vision, talent, innovation, execution, and commitment. This

113

book shows you how to bring it all together to become a powerfully positive leader.

www.powerofpositiveleadership.com

The Energy Bus Field Guide

The Energy Bus Field Guide is your roadmap to fueling your life, work, and team with positive energy. The international bestseller, *The Energy Bus*, has helped millions of people from around the world shift to a more positive outlook. This guide is a practical companion to help you *live and share* the ten principles from *The Energy Bus* every day, with real, actionable steps you can immediately put into practice in your life, work, team, and organization.

The Power of a Positive Team

In *The Power of a Positive Team*, Jon Gordon draws upon his unique team building experience, as well as conversations with some of the greatest teams in history, to provide an essential framework of proven practices to empower teams to work together more effectively and achieve superior results.

www.PowerOfAPositiveTeam.com

The Coffee Bean

From bestselling author Jon Gordon and rising star Damon West comes *The Coffee Bean:* an illustrated fable that teaches readers how to transform their environment, overcome challenges, and create positive change.

The Energy Bus for Kids

The illustrated children's adaptation of the bestselling book, *The Energy Bus*, tells the story of George, who, with the help of his school bus driver, Joy, learns that if he believes in himself, he'll find the strength to overcome any challenge. His journey teaches kids how to overcome negativity, bullies, and everyday challenges to be their best.

www.EnergyBusKids.com

Thank You and Good Night

Thank You and Good Night is a beautifully illustrated book that shares the heart of gratitude. Jon Gordon takes a little boy and girl on a fun-filled journey from one perfect moonlit night to the next. During their adventurous days and nights, the children explore the people, places, and things they are thankful for.

The Hard Hat for Kids

The Hard Hat for Kids is an illustrated guide to teamwork. Adapted from the bestseller *The Hard Hat*, this uplifting story presents practical insights and life-changing lessons that are immediately applicable to everyday situations, giving kids—and adults—a new outlook on cooperation, friendship, and the selfless nature of true teamwork.

www.HardHatforKids.com